Xanthippe and Her Friends

☙

Beate Sigriddaughter

FUTURECYCLE PRESS
www.futurecycle.org

Library of Congress Control Number: 2017964649

Published by FutureCycle Press
Athens, Georgia, USA

ISBN 978-1-942371-46-5

Dedicated to Xanthippe

Xanthippe was the not exactly beloved wife
of the revered philosopher Socrates. For a long time
her name was used as a synonym for shrew.

Having lived for many years among wise
and also unwise men, I want to honor her memory,
together with the memory of all women, sung or unsung,
who have bravely made and continue to make their way
through this complicated existence of questionable attitudes
with grace and rage and sadness and joy.

Contents

Part IV

Thirteen Love Poems and Twelve Songs of Despair

Part I

Xanthippe and Her Friends

Xanthippe

Today the light of daisies is exuberant.
I saw three goslings in the sea. I am
in love – this world: The lilacs are almost
done. The poppies have begun. The veils
of willows, sun-drenched, billow over grass.
Without the bats and the lupines, truth is
expensive and irrelevant. The blue bells
will prevail, the foxes. I forgive you,
Socrates, for choosing hemlock.

The Storyteller

Today I crown myself Sheherazade
in that part of me will listen,
always, to the king. I hear

I am slow but do not stutter,
even when he rises
with irrefutable logic, meting out
the judgment: I must die.

And so I will
meet death in his time
with life on my lips,

like a spring humming over
the leaden drought of rock, rapidly
in the slow rock-reshaping
wending of her way

or like a music rising
from her jubilant elaboration
loose over the rock-beat of rhythm,

for this earth is not
a destiny of silence, though impatient
death imposes
ropes of better worlds to come, or none.

Let the earth and her stories
recall me to themselves.

Neruda's Mermaid

(a companion piece to Pablo Neruda's
"Fable of the Mermaid and the Drunks")

No, I am not a mermaid,
and I do have speech
and clothes to cover me.
Other than that, I am
as lost as his mermaid
in a world of men too drunk
with competitive contempt
to notice eyes the color
of distant love. Easier by far
to egg each other on
to blacken me with mockery
and cigarette butts and
whatever else is at hand.
And I know I must leave
through that door somehow
and swim toward the
emptiness that frightens me –
it is so vast – and swim toward
my death that frightens me –
it comes so soon.
The emptiness frightens me
more – I wanted to make
something with my lovely
white arms, but I need them
for swimming away.

The Wedding: Snow White

I'm not out of the woods yet.
Those brambles were nothing.
That hissing and howling
and hooting at night – nothing compared
with my stunned innocence.

I dreamed, like all girls,
of my dance in white satin, never this:
at my wedding celebration my unsuccessful
stepmom is condemned to dance
to her death on heated iron slippers.
They are bringing them in now
with smoking tongs.

Someone hands me a glass. I take it
with my habitual champagne grace.
I am confused here. Am I
to gloat and triumph and rejoice?

No wonder Prince Charming didn't take
our dance lessons seriously. He knew
I wouldn't be so keen on dancing ever after.
How am I to enjoy my wedding night
with this orgy of vengeance still fresh
on my mind?

It's not that I condone
eating your stepchild's liver and heart,
or poisoning the competition. I don't
like competition in the first place,
the greedy marketing of mirrors, selling
seductive beauty at any price, and then
condemning the loser to blistering death.

Here are my choices. Gloat and rejoice,
dilute myself with drink or Disney bliss,
or stand up to my true self at last, white
as a sheet, or my dress, oh, yes, or snow.

I clink the side of my glass, at least
no longer a coffin. That's something.

The princess wishes to speak.
This wedding is cancelled
until we find a better way.
Any woman's dishonor diminishes me.

Sappho

You may forget but
let me tell you this:
someone in some future time
will think of us
–Sappho

I am grateful to the hands
that snatched the small remaining
fragments from the blazing library
in Alexandria

I am grateful to the many hands
including mine that copied
words into this future now

you cannot simply burn the past
and expect it to stay burned forever

it lives like the memory of reptiles
crawling to land to breathe
for the first time air

it lives like this one in a garland
of poets climbing to breathe
astonished for the first time
love

Eurydice

Among shamans they tell this
as a joke, that Orpheus was merely
one of them who went down
to the underworld and failed
to guide a vanished soul back into life,
probably dawdled, took notes on despair,
and disregarded all rules.
Now I too have gone for you,
though my poems are not nearly
as sweet as his songs, and the gods
we nowadays keep not nearly as obliging.
I had one advantage, though:
I am a woman, not a fool.
If they tell me the important thing is
not to look back, I do not look
back. You can make it alone through this
maze of spiritual hiding. I know
there are doubts. You may have
already forgotten all earthly things.
But earth is here, and life is
here. I can't look back now, my love,
oh my love. I don't know
where you are, woman, or who
anymore. I must take this on trust.
It is not easy. If you can live again,
I will meet you where the sun is rising.

The Wanderers

Do you remember scenes we passed
on roads we never traveled?
I meant to wear two skirts and have you
paint me as a gypsy.

I remember the poppy fields I wasn't
born to see. Your father's wagon
broke across the hill at dawn:
poppies, orange, and sun.

I remember songs I promised and never
had time to write. They are growing,
Eurydice. Soon they will fall into rhythm
or cliffs lined with agave.

I will not pray that we meet again:
Those roads are already rolling. But I hope
and pray down peace all night,
for you, beloved, for me.

And as the sun's dust awakens to dance,
peace comes, no matter what road I lie on.

Like a Prince

I have acted like a prince much
of my life, never mind my gender.
I removed your obstacles as others
kill dragons. And when I came down
from the mountain, still covered in sweat
and mist and dragon blood and the sweet
sense of triumph, you, like a princess, had
a haircut appointment with Pierre
at eleven forty-five and it just wouldn't do
to offend him by making a change. I watched
you choose sun block and count French fries,
and I think I will go back up the mountain
and find another dragon. Maybe
this one I will feed and tame.

The Empty Pedestal

"...but it was a big pedestal,
and you could move freely;
why did you have to climb down?"

He mumbled something about draft
and marble and cold feet.

Poem Containing "So," "And," "Such"

And so they said the heavy usage of
such words as "so" and "and" and "such"
always gives away a woman writer,
also known as poetess. And we all know
what that means, do we not? A trifle
sentimental, and so personal, and so much love.
So that I studiously wanted to avoid
such easy giveaways so very much.

And then I had my first poems, so
belabored, relatively free of "so"
and "and" and "such." And I was married then,
and so I went to ask my husband once:
"Tell me, why is it that my women friends
always like my writing so much better
than do any of the men (whom,
in parentheses, I'm begging to approve)?"
And he said, cautiously, he didn't know.

And so I had to ask myself
such questions over and over and over again,
until I had no choice but to grow up
with them into the shape of my own answer.

And frankly,
I would rather be a goddess than a god,
and so I must conclude
that I would rather be a poetess
than ever again a poet, straining hard
against my being, merely to avoid
such words as "so" and "and" and "such."

The Tightrope Walker's Demonstration

"I declare that it's all a matter of

trust," she mumbled, rubbing her knees,
looking up at the slackened rope,
then at the concerned young man by the tree
who had so skillfully unwound it.

"Oh, abracadabra," she muttered, losing
her first limp toward the tree, and tying
all the knots again. She swung herself
into the proper branch, and in grand manner
threw into the audience a fragment
of torn lace that had been trailing
from the outer layer of her skirts.

"It's all a matter of trust," she declared
and danced her way into the well-strung line.
And as she did a cartwheel in the center,
the confused young man cried out:
"Lady, I was only worried. If you had to
fall, I wanted you to do so early,
when the risks were relatively mild.
Not later on. Not now."

"Thank you, young man," she called down with a bow,
then, taking her good time, she danced along
into the open arms of the opposite tree.

When Lightning Strikes Men

When lightning strikes men, women beware!
Saul turns into Paul. Once playboy, now he declares
women off limits and men their head.
Luther turns from celibate monk to marriage
and proclaims that women have broader hips
so as to better sit on them at home while men
conduct importance elsewhere in the world.
Augustine, story has it, only sees lightning strike
something else. It affects him all the same.
Formerly playboy, too, he now pens spicy diatribes.
He knows whereof he speaks, condemning
women for having these beautiful bodies,
or even ugly ones, for that matter, inciting such
vicious and indomitable lust in men,
which bodies, even though their owners have no souls
and are stupid and useless, they nevertheless connived
to create purposely for the downfall of men,
just like Eve once frivolously fed an apple to Adam.
Because, you see, God created everything
except apparently women's bodies, for which they are
entirely themselves to blame. God would have never
fashioned anything that vexing and demoralizing
to the peace of the stalwart masters of the universe.
Amen.

Amo Ergo Sum: I Love Therefore I Am

I love

to run in late-October morning light
full moon to my west full
sun to my east gold aspen
showers whispering down in this last
dry wind before snow

  she sat on the edge of his bed
  tendrils of dawn reached through
  milk white curtains for her hair
  falling softly she was putting
  on something a sock a shoe
  and looked up without speaking
  like a doe disturbed at her grass

I run I pray through tears I touch
cottonwood dashed by a night gust
a stalk of wild wheat a long blade
of grass I pick up a handful of sand

  he was blocked from vision
  all but his toes was he smiling
  astonished not yet awake to all
  the complications of her being
  half my age and he my husband
  and I in the doorway breathless

I think of Hera endlessly embarrassed
by Zeus and his amorous ways
swans heifers and rage as though
his needs were always our shame

  I imagine him tomorrow sighing to his pals
  but I didn't even do anything no
  nothing really she was just
  sitting there and his friends
  full of advice buy roses lie low

in stride my breath catches
sun moon of course I love
this wealth of life and beauty and
the two of them are part of it
and smaller than I feared

as mist curls into day
where all that has the courage
to be and the chance is stunning

and sun glints on muscle and desire
to go deeper into words and destiny
like Michelangelo cutting at marble
to meet his angels in the stone I love

therefore I am

Escape Literature

The world is all that is the case.
–Ludwig Wittgenstein

She laughed and held out her arms to him.
–Nora Roberts

There's Wittgenstein, and he will take you
on semantic roller-coaster
dips of language to that magic place
of intellectual self-pleasure. You
might even go all the way
to nirvana. It's only a synapse further
up the reality escape: a steel
contraption all the way to heaven,
radiating ice across existence.

Then there is Nora Roberts: lush
caress with feather-brush desire to
stay here, embrace, and celebrate
life, samsara, until
you wonder why
they call this escape for those
who prefer to not go with the master
exodus of Wittgenstein's Houdini fans,
dancing on logistics into nothingness,
respectably in Finnegan's wake. Until

the question begs itself:
Who exactly does the escaping?

Anxiety

Horned lizard, young
and concerned
with a flat worried mouth

reminds me how
I hear, and get, the
trendy advice:
Love yourself.

But deep within me
is an ancient fear
that loving myself
simply won't count.

And God, invoked
for all-purpose
love, turns out to be
too distant for comfort.

Would you please
dance with me, if only
just a little?

Part II

The Laughter of Grass

Angel Loop, September

In Canto 30 of *Paradiso,* Dante
sings of the laughter of grass.
I am almost there now. Running
on Angel Loop, I rub shoulders
with tall mountain marigold
and goldeneye, a festival
of yellow, some blue
trumpet shapes, some red.
My favorite bald rock stretches
steep into the yellow. Yesterday
I tickled grass. I wanted to
hear laughter, but it was just
crickets rubbing legs in the wind.
I will likely never understand
why we need darkness when
we yearn and strive for light. I get
the concept of duality. Only my heart
is obstinate and wishes to believe
pure light is possible. Meanwhile
a lizard dives face first under
a ledge as I ponder scorpions
and roses. I wish the lizards trusted me.
To them I am one of the shadows
of darkness. Still I want to belong
to light, to laughter, to lizards
believing in love. Today
grass tickled me. There are asters too
now, yellow centers full of summer
scent and whispering goodbye.

A Fable of Leaves

Imagine
one precocious leaf,
in late August, turning
conscious of itself and
how the tree, the mother
tree, all spring, all summer
long poured sap,
bearing in patience
the weight.

You know the rest,
something like a religious
movement among autumnal trees,
leaves considerately turning
weightless, singing eerie
mantras in the wind.

And the mother tree
whose effortless
spill was living wine
considers burden, agrees
and urges no more
strength into veins needing
less, then nothing,
nirvana fluttering
in glowing sainthood
to the dust
and the delight of children.

But the pine trees continue
less spectacular,
claiming no season
for death,
the needles hanging on
to life without clamor
or applause or shame,
piercing winter's
lace of snow with evergreen.

Cathedral Garden

she walks through
the mist of perceptions of
the texture of previous
lives brushed from her
mind in the harvest of feeling
not yet intact her eyes
searching among the heavy
angels half blind with pressure
of now the yellow image of
a tarot card a falcon trapped
and feeding on her hand
grapes in the background no
not grapes gray angels
the city below the space of
now again with its burdens
lust pressure sex
the whirlpool of what
could be should be dragging
her beyond the cross of Latin
words drifting low
in the mélange smoke lights
pollution windows falling deeper
dawn fusing distant stones
as the breath of the wind
welds sunlight to her skin
her spine incandescence
the lives not stuttering stone
angel phrases but breathing
through her blood the stunning
silence this
I always will be here

Archer

She has always wanted to belong. Now
it looks like she does. Dad offers
a sip of his beer. She giggles, shakes
her head. Heartthrob Rogelio nods;
his dark eyes gleam with admiration. First
time he looks at her like that. Nobody
says the dread words, "for a girl."
The men offer to skin and gut
the deer. She ponders this, accepts.
She still feels the sinew of the bow,
her strong and steady arms, the whistle
and velocity of death. The wounded eyes
film over, lifeless, without accusation.
"Well done," someone says. She wants
to ask back: "Have you ever looked
into the eyes of a deer?" Their calm
and dark acceptance, shy round
innocence with just a hint of question.
And the bold nose. But no words come.
She is in a different league now.
Tomorrow she will be sixteen.
They promise her first taste
of the meat. She feels empty, silenced,
betrayed. No one explained triumph
would feel like this. She remembers
wide surprise in eyes so black that
they could make you weep. The finches
in the juniper have lost their charm.

Caged Light

You want to control
the seed, the womb. You can't
even master your own lust.

Then you dismantle
the children. Illegitimate,
you throw them away
where they swell in shame
and confusion and foam
across the globe.

I am caged
light. You know
what that means. Yes
you do. I will show you
illegitimate dolphins and
the bottom line of roses.

Pine Siskin

"Look," I murmured to the green bird crashed
on the balcony and filling half my hand now. "The forest
is still there. You can make it. You still know how."

The bird sat motionless. Only its beak opened
and closed without sound. A downy tuft
of yellow and white stuck sideways from its wing.

I stroked its head with one finger. It kept opening
and closing its beak without sound. From time to time
a slow film of blinking moved down its eye.

From inside the closed balcony door the cat watched
with surprising calm. My heartbeat too was calm.
For a short while I knew everything, with certainty.

"You can do this," I murmured over and over and over,
and when the green bird flew into the nearest tree, which was
indeed still there, I knew I had been talking to myself.

Midsummer Night's Wake

1.
Nothing has died
except my cancerous ambition.

2.
I stay awake at the window
through the last glimmer of light
though it is not clear
when it comes. Eventually it is mostly dark
except for the glow of the village below.
I have vowed to honor each last
nuance of shimmer, and if it is no longer
the sun but the town instead, I will
honor that too.

I have been betrayed,
cheated of some of the best moments
of my life so far. I promise to change this,
not myself, no, but the constant
harshness of conformity.

I listen to sweet music as I honor the light.
Later I will not remember what that music is.
It is pretty, but not as important
as the pulse of my soul. My love
is important, my yearning, the exact love
I've let myself be talked out of
in the name of respectability.

3.
It was the longest day
of the year.

I think of my first love who once wrote
in a letter: "This young man did well for
himself," as he got honors, but also betrayals,
from a world that praised his intellect and
claimed his body for war.

I too have done well in your world, my love,
I played quite well in it, only I never
belonged. And perhaps you did not
either as your body crumpled around
your astonishing brain.

I'm determined to walk home now,
limping a little from all the falseness,
all the breaking.

4.

Believe me, when something
miraculous happens, like a sip
of champagne or a forget-me-not
among the roses, don't try to repeat it.
Simply bow to miracles.
Savor them as I savor the light.

I remember spending other
midsummer nights staying late
at the office, collating last minute
FedExes for the bottom line.

I will no longer be betrayed.
At least not voluntarily. At least
not for praise or overtime pay.

5.

I am not Athena, sprung
from Daddy's brain. Or am I?
With my fears, my fairness, my
obedience.

I am not Cassandra, praying
to Athena in vain: Shelter me, don't let him
drag me away to be raped, don't,
oh, goddess, don't let this last piece
of humiliation of all that is life happen
to me.
          Or am I? Dragged out

into the rat race as fodder for
immeasurable greed.

I am both and neither, sitting crouched
in the corner, huddled around
the sorrow of my soul.

I cannot promise that you will
not again be betrayed, my soul,
but I promise the one betraying you
from here on out will not be me.

I will be the one sheltering you, doing
my best, building higher sanctuary walls,
if necessary, telling you it is all right, for I
will cradle you through the last glimmer of light,
through the last flicker of life
with a fox's vast talent for invisibility
despite its great beauty.

If anyone sees you, it will be someone
who knows or yearns to know
how to love, how to treasure
the great romance of life.

Century Plant

When conditions are right, it begins
to lift fantastic energy
out of its plump circle of leaves,
a bump first, then a stalk
that grows, inches each day,
to tower over ten feet tall.
Yellow buds open, stamens
like snake tongues tasting the air,
sneak out and turn into trays
of buzzing celebration.

I was warned. The bloom completed,
the plant is done and simply dies.
Still when the circle of succulent green
leaves at the bottom paled, announcing
all the energy was spent, I grew sad.

For many years tall ghosts stand still,
gray now, and dry, a shelter for birds,
a camouflage for lizards on the prowl,
lifeless monuments to life. In the wind
last year's ghost pods whisper
instructions to this year's growth.

When she lost her mother
at age four, my own mother asked:
"Who will now give us our bread?"
Meanwhile she has fed me far beyond
the day she said she was tired,
wanted to sleep and didn't wake up.
I am well nourished. This year,
had she lived, she would be more
than a century old. She whispers
instructions. I want to caress
her spirit with a language of

somersaults, a memory of yellow
flowers buzzing with brief celebration.

I wish we could all live forever.

Woman at the Crossroad

She walks in beauty, yearns
in peace, grows lilacs and roses,
sometimes picks forget-me-nots
down by the river, and knows
that deer can sound like women
talking, but wants to keep this
a secret from hunters, of course.

She lives alone, loves solitude.
Her thick white hair hangs
down to her waist. One day
her window is broken. There
wasn't much to steal. Her laptop
is gone. Her eyes ache.

Another woman recommends a gun.
"Here, hold mine, see how it feels."
She doesn't believe in guns.
She doesn't even believe in high heels.
Her eyebrows contract.
She hesitates.

Yearning To Praise

Beauty starts so early: a bowl of roses
at the inn, sunrise with my father
at the lake. A sailboat crosses liquid orange.
Blue beads of glass glide through
my fingers like desire. I am

filled with gratitude. The green scent of rain.
Discord, of course. First: "You're only a girl."
Later high praise: "You think like a man." I am
drenched with hunger. I have learned to live
with it. Magenta desert bloom. At night

the breathless stars. Surely I was meant to be
a comet. There, a red-winged blackbird. Red-
winged grasshoppers too, psychedelic, blazing
sunsets, roses in spring and after the monsoon
again. I am grateful. Sun scent on wood and dust.

Another woman in another desert is silenced
with stones for angering men, not a thousand
years ago, not even a hundred, but yesterday.
She thought she was safe and honored,
as we so often do. I send belated, useless love.

So I will praise magenta desert bloom and
some brave journalists who will not let me
sleep. Three peaches on my tree this year,
and lizards sunning on stone. Roses again,
as gratitude and hungry prayer tear at me.

Ceremony

This is who I am,
arms crossed, braced
against the morning
cold, waiting for
the sun.

Parts of me long
to kneel
to pray, to spread
my arms
wide open in
some ancient
ritual.

In my many years
on earth
I have not found
a single
ceremony
that does not
discourage
women
or dogs, or both.

Here by the cactus
and shrub oak
all are welcome,
honored. Deer
stroll by,
a raven's wings
stir the air,
and, yes,
from time to time
a neighbor's dog,
tan, saunters
into morning.

Then suddenly the sun
pierces the hill
on the horizon,
as always brilliantly
indifferent.

And so I vow
to do my breathless
best with all
this beauty
and exuberance.

Even in winter
I stand, casual,
hands in my pocket,
wool up to my eyes,
still braced against
the world.

But I come
each morning
to pray
like this, for this
is who I am.

Part III

Dona Nobis Pacem

Pieta

I.

A woman at work solicits paperbacks
for our soldiers, especially action/suspense.

I feel for her, wanting to help, yet
here I sit trapped in my white marble grief
for our sons that are always so broken.

Often it feels we lose our men
long before they enlist in their dreams
of glory that we haven't healed
in more than ten thousand years.

II.

In Papua New Guinea women make a pact
to slay their male babies, as there seems
to be no other way to stop a brutal war
of already far too many generations.

At this point men in the west are crying "murder."
Would you rather wait till they all grow up
and kill each other properly then?

III.

In Israel they are willing to imprison
high school kids who do not want to
kill and do not want to die.

IV.

You say it is too difficult to simply withdraw
and let go of righteous dreams.
You say I don't understand the staggering
complexities.

Do you believe that it is easier to simply die?

V.

Come home, my love, and live.

I want you in the fields beside me,
not huddling in faraway trenches. I want you
to climb with me the narrow path toward
intelligence with its dangerous cliffs
and its breathtaking vistas.

I don't want you on my lap,
broken for any reason.

Come home, my son, my brother,
my father, my husband.
Come home, my love, and live.

September 11, 2001

A silver slice
a litany of blood
the rubble of severed futures

hard to hear what is holy
through jackhammer sirens of greed
inflamed testosterone
that werewolf lust of power
forgive us God for

we were meant to build
you and for each of us
a future worth living

we mourn instead
the beauty we have lost
the purposeful and smiling names
of loss like prayer beads
nodes on our DNA together with
the shreds of plasma
that fiercely believed
in a hero's reception with Allah

we turn our eyes with hope
with shame to celebrate again
the sacred trust of life
that we were meant to be

November 30, 2003: Iraq

(two days after Bush opted to serve
Thanksgiving turkey to his troops in Iraq,
there was a major massacre)

How many women are weeping tonight,
clenching their hearts in despair
over the shreds of husbands they have
lately kissed, lovers and sons they have
cradled, now feasted on by flies?

If someone had slain my lover last night,
my heart would shriek into a thousand pieces,
would slash at all life with the blood
beat stop of disbelief. I can feel their raw
hearts pumping, unbridled, in mine.

And I stagger here for the love
they can no longer feel,
begging you, world, for peace.

Valhalla

Welcome to our sacred hall
for warriors slain in battle,
this male paradise designed uniquely
to find feast and fight for all
eternity.

Each day you get to rise to battle
again all gory day long, better
than football, complete with blood,
severed limbs, steel through the heart,
spilled brains, to be revived
in time for revelry at night
at Odin's table, pork and mead
dished out by glorious maidens.

Admission is a violent demise
which melds you to irrevocable
masculinity, a sort of graduate program
in destruction. You can major in
methods for killing, the arts
of slaughter or brutality and rape,
and so much more.

Despite the pork we don't discriminate
on grounds of religion. We cater to all
disciples of death.

First envisioned as a consolation prize
for loss of life and limb, we have become
by far the most popular segment of heaven.

Some give it all their lives.

Burning

(Zimbabwe 1980)

I remember the night we went into the fields
to show our solidarity with the Zimbabwe
students celebrating their ancient country's
brand-new independence by raising
the new flag into the night wind,
lowering the old accompanied by some
haphazard singing. Most didn't yet know
the new national anthem, if there was one
already; the rest were above
such frivolous considerations. There was
no lack of beer and cheap wine and girls'
voices and young men's voices.
I felt honored to be there
until the old flag had come down
and a young man improvised a scream
of loud obligatory hatred: BURN THEM!
BURN OUR ENEMIES! BURN OUR OPPRESSORS! LIKE THIS!
He leapt for the flag in the grass
and with his colonial cigarette lighter
he set its edges on fire.

I remember the shiver and the distancing
in me; first everything reeled
and gave way, and then I was back
home in my native German body. I do not remember
the smell of burning human flesh. I do not
remember the sound, but I can recognize any echo.
BURN THEM! BURN OUR ENEMIES, OUR POWERFUL WOMEN!
BURN THE WITCHES! BURN THEM! BURN
OUR ENEMIES, OUR TEACHERS! BURN THE JEWS!

And I long in no facile fashion,
since I too have murder in my genes,
for a time when human lust was sated
– we had come so far once – with burning

effigies of winter, carried with shrieks
and blood-curdling music, drums,
down to the narrow river that flows, dragging
the flaming puppets of straw down its eddies,
lapping the borders of fields in their green,
mirroring the moon only, and no sacrifice
or vengeance in anyone's heart.

That Day

that day
I woke up wanting to caress
the face of things
to whisper
to live is enough

that day
I rode a fairground ride in celebration
sky blue Denver tilting
and a small boy by my side
kissing the whirlwind with laughter

that day
I learned that scientists are working
on a bomb that vaporizes
human life on impact
finding us by body heat
leaving the more valuable things
unharmed the buildings
intact the roads the bridges

not even in my dreams had I been
this breathless against my will

for whom
will these bridges span?
will the books then read themselves?
for whom will roller coasters roll?

that day
I vowed to quick
caress this sweet quick world
without pity without promise
but with a passion that

even a single soldier rolling
in the dirt of conflict would be more

sacred than a bridge a drop of oil
an ocean of democracy

there will be no more tears then
quick now caress

Gratia Plena

all prayer in the end is gratitude
without exception shells wait to be sand
as life recycles poems at my feet in purple
moist exuberance while seagulls practice solos
with wings made transparent by sunrise

yes in the morning the crows fly west
and east again at night I love that
everyone is so busy being alive heartbreaking
even the sound of water on pebbles receding
click click turning stones into music

a heron fishes precise in his hunger
he takes no more from the sea than he needs
though the lush orange and yellow maple leaves
some larger than my hand whisper there's more
and a flower flickers white behind a vine

if life has petals that large what can it
possibly not do despite the wars we conduct
or tolerate or do not speak against or not loudly
enough afraid of miracles we avoid the eyes
of all angels we try to nail down death first

rather than open hands to life the uncharted
the unfamiliar the patient courtship that begs
to listen to pray with each footfall to praise
and to believe it possible to change the world
by trailing a grateful hand in water

Alchemist

Lovely woman,
amber light
pouring liquids
through new filters,
love shimmers
blue in her hands,
sparks so vivid
under her touch.
It is time
for peace.

Part IV

Thirteen Love Poems
and Twelve Songs of Despair

Desire

First Love Poem

Where do I begin?

My parents whisper
in ways I cannot imagine.
A birth with snow and candlelight
is easier to grasp.

We all come from desire.
Desire trumps wisdom.

Your long dark hair fanned out
across my threadbare clean sheets, you
so in love so many years ago
even my cigarette mouth
didn't matter. We cannot go back,
not ever, though in dreams
I go from time to time.

Now, so much older, I walk down
a dry riverbed with you. I carry
some of your stuff into the wilderness
you have chosen.

Farewell, my love. There are places
we must walk alone. It is difficult
to say goodbye between stone
walls, juniper, and primrose. You
in your plaid shirt and wide-rim hat
against the sun whom we both love
but also respect in the desert
midday.

Be well, my love, in the wild
places you belong. Soon
you will sleep under stars. One day
you will take me with you
to the places you belong.

Oh, one more kiss, so soft, then off
in different directions, you
to the beauty of your wilderness, I
to the beauty of my words.
One more curve
in the riverbed, one more wave
goodbye; my love, we have chosen,
you that, I this.

On the way out I get lost.
Not long, it is all so obvious
when you pay attention.

Later that day I dream I am lost.
At times you are with me. Maybe
this way? At times I am alone.
Maybe that? I know I am going
in the right direction, but I am plagued
with gnats of impatience and
a wish for effortless perfection.

Perhaps the best part of my dream?
I didn't mind being lost.
It was interesting. I was focused.

But in reality I do not stay lost.
The way is past the alligator log,
then through the saddle between
two gentle hills; follow the crest
of a ridge, yes, then finally the cairn
just beyond the Indian paintbrush
that luckily no deer has eaten,
then home where I find
I love you.

And I never want to leave
or change
this gentle place of knowing.

Patriarchy

First Song of Despair

It is not your fault
you were taught love is,
for a man, undignified.

It is not my fault
I was unable to compellingly
inspire otherwise.

It is not our fault
we landed in a world
where we poison each other
for profit.

The bitterness of plastic
exploitation frightens me.

How can we straighten
the future with one
of us cautioned against
feeling, the other
warned against
unfolding?

Strange things are
encouraged to grow out
of proportion
while both of us
proudly defend
our crippled stance.

How do we get
out of here, crippled
like this?

Fairy Tale

Second Love Poem

In a fairy tale the princess decides
to build a golden road and declares
whoever comes down the middle
is the one.

It is true, wrong princes see gold
and think it would be such a shame
to damage it. Her true love doesn't
even notice. He is thinking only
of her and how he will be
with her soon.

I did notice when I left many
things I owned behind
to be with you. Sometimes
their memory still tugs at me.

Still, bravely, I have always been
part knight, part damsel.
When my heart first broke
open for you, unicorns spilled out
and foxes, flame-framed glimpses
of light, heat, sunrays, flickering.

I had a vision once. The two of us
climbed up into the sun
on a long ladder of ribbons.
There we sat side by side and looked,
content, into the world.

I was raised on fairy tales, sweet
ginger feelings, crystal moods.
They nourish me still. Tell me
the part again where you will be
my love forever.

Back in the Woods

Second Song of Despair

I am so crippled by importance,
basic masculine addiction to politics and other
serious things. Money. Competition.
Sex.

We're still in the woods here,
though the princess has long left,
and I am her helpless, not unpleasant
shell.

You don't even notice in all this
chaos of significance. For all you know
she is still in the garden, playing
her flute.

I wonder what would have become of me
had I remained informed by news
instead of poetry. Khrushchev, Adenauer,
de Gaulle.

Decades later men still meet in the dark
important suits, whether I am
informed or not, while they commission
war

and gadgets of insinuated peace
and other promises, then store abandoned
contracts underground. I cannot compete
with this.

Perhaps this is the secret message
of a fairy tale: The princess does nothing
and still love falls where it will. Or
she departs unnoticed.

A Book of Love

Third Love Poem

I want to live the book of love
for you. It is all I have
always wanted. I am a bit afraid
of its uncanny silence.

I feel suddenly naked, as though
I have never lived before
and a huge wave of surrender
laps at my feet, sweeter
than flute song, darker
than my often brutal tenderness,
like earth surprised at the beauty
of her own sunsets.

When I was very young
I confidently wanted to become
a poet. I thought I would do
nothing but love and sing and praise.
Was I ever surprised. Still,
I have done well
enough. I carried love to safety
through the complicated landscapes
of our lives.

I want to give you everything
my soul can spare. My life, yes.
Everything I own, which isn't all
that much. Once, on the way
from our wedding at the waterfall,
I gave you all the wild flowers
on the steep trail down. You were
happy when you realized
I meant to leave them all in place.

The one thing I cannot give you is
my soul itself, but you knew that.
Here is the key to it for those times
when you are not too busy
with the splendor of your own.

Jealousy

Third Song of Despair

I am jealous of everything
that stirs you more than I do,
everything that kindles light

in your beautiful eyes:
your best friend on the phone,
two exciting women

back from hiking the entire
Continental Divide Trail,
far more riveting than I

with my roses and my poems.
And then eagles, flying snakes, and
– how utterly embarrassing –

barnacles. I mean, barnacles!
The message I hear is: "Get back
in line. No exceptions for you."

It feels like untimely snow when
all the leaves are out and early roses
quiver, smashed against the ground.

Your Beautiful Eyes

Fourth Love Poem

Foxes have a lot to say
if you listen. One
keeps reminding me how
down in the canyon
the river flows
not because it is loved,
but because it must.

The mere thought of the river
reminds me of course of
those many years ago, how
your eyes, intense from rapids,
changed for me suddenly,
fierce and soft all at once,
like the first jolt of sunlight
piercing the already shimmering
edge of morning.

Though the river was
dangerous and gorgeous, I too
was suddenly
important in your world.

I was already in love when
that moment flooded me forever
with significance and hunger
for impossible completion.

I had always imagined love
would look like that.

Attention

Fourth Song of Despair

It feels like a great blindness
has settled on the land.
I grope around and suspect
you notice me most unhappy.
You pay attention then.
When I am angry, though,
you really notice. It is a wonder
I am not raging all the time.

A tiny consolation:
how we take the sun for granted
too, and gravity. Nature is
indifferent. By nature. But you,
with you I dreamed of wandering
side by side, confirming
our exquisite place in this
maelstrom of molecules
in the whirling of stars.

I want my small exception
without having to remind you.
I want to rekindle
your eyes. It is wrong to be
listless and blind and hungry.

The time of the lioness has come.

Crystals

Fifth Love Poem

You are, yes,
kin to river otters
but also to rock.
Once in a distant
country you took
a stone from a
mountain. Later
you felt its wish
to be returned
and you hiked
many hours
to take it home.

You are so kind.

I know about
desire. Once I left
a tantalizing crystal
on a mountain top
where it belonged
knowing I would
never find another
like it. It still dazzles
me in dreams and
shimmers in regret.

Desire means
approximately
"from the stars."
Desire is my home.
You touch me
like flame,
like cool water.

Respect and Love

Fifth Song of Despair

We travel in a world seeded
by men's ancient prayers
thanking their convenient God for
not having created them women.

Look at these flowers, then,
boys on the playground,
mechanics, teachers, plasterers,
lawyers, miners, glassblowers,
coffee shop owners, engineers,
doctors, fathers, sons, all
swaggering in their relief at being
superior to the likes of me at least.

Sometimes they sweep me
a bow of such benevolent contempt.

And I stand there, a red-faced girl,
screaming my ineffectual tantrum,
collapsing at last in a heap of grief,
raw in my stolen innocence.

One day, when I am quite old,
I stand up again and look
at my incredible limbs, my skin.
I taste my lips. Life whistles
like a breeze: See how far
you came anyway?
You did not need respect or love
to get here at all. Yes, but

I whisper back. Thank you
for beauty and for breath,
for the sleek mountain paths,
the mists, the lizards of early morning
who also need neither love nor respect.

But do you ever, life, dream with me
how beautiful it could have been?

Aubade

Sixth Love Poem

Dawn is again, somehow
that is significant.

Dawn is again,
perhaps it always is.

Dawn is again,
and I still hear you.

Dawn is the hour
of children grown too old
to sleep through a peace like this.

I say: Your shadow is exquisite.
You say: But in this shadow is no face.
What would you want with a face
at this hour?

All enemies are unconvincing
and strangers live only by daylight.

But this is dawn,
and I know you still.

Bricks

Sixth Song of Despair

Silence.

There are things we must not say.

There was a time when the law said
a woman who speaks out
against a man shall have her mouth
crushed with fire bricks.

There was a time when the law said
adulterers must be bound
and thrown in the river, even
a woman who was raped.
Her husband could pull her out
of the river, if he so desired,
while the king himself
could save a man he valued.

I am tired and heavy with things
I must not say. This silence slides
like grains of broken brick
between my teeth.

Arthur, with affectionate regret,
did not choose Guinevere
over law or flames. Would you
pull me from the river
if they tossed me there
against my will?
That is the question.

Oh, I remember: I am not
supposed to take things personally.
But I am the daughter of daughters
of women who were miraculously
neither drowned nor burned.

They have trained me with such memory
that you no longer have to crush
my mouth with bricks. All you have
to do is look at me a certain way.

This silence is not easy to undo.
How I hate this silence.

A Better Silence

Seventh Love Poem

There is a better silence. This,
like a secret, I would like to keep

unchanged. Drops glisten
on a blade of grass, a bird
high in the tree, first opening
its throat, then closing it again
in the chapel of new dawn,
to save its song for later.

Your eyes are open. And my heart
is filled with darklight flickering.
History's beguiling whisper falls
away, the future is forgotten,
and the world sleeps naked,
innocently dreaming of itself,
the silk of skin, the hush of sun
on wood and earth
and you.

Excuses

Seventh Song of Despair

I hear our cry for love, like
children having learned
the stern mechanics of attention.
If we are sick, we can collect.
Pain is honored. Dead,
we would finally be missed,
though perhaps not enough.
We can never be sure of

enough. We call ourselves
unworthy and hope for God
and the world to disagree, and
to invite us back into the center
of the universe,

especially our complicated God
whom we appointed purposely
to be sure of someone's love
out there, for loving yourself,
though highly recommended,
never seems adequate.

And so I sacrifice and ache
and moan to dramatize to you
my merits in the field of love.

Do I claim love then as – what
would you call it – an excuse for
not doing something with my life?

And what exactly is it I would do?

Lord of Lizards

Eighth Love Poem

When I am in danger
of forgetting the beauty
of it all, I look at the fence
where I once spotted
a lizard in the sun, quite large,
with turquoise belly skin,
and, on second look,
trapped in fine wire,
unable to move.

We trembled
as you slowly cut mesh
around the tiny claws,
the scaly neck, the limbs.
It took a long time.
We didn't expect the lizard
to make it. Still,
you carried it
into the shade.

It didn't move. We tried
to give it water
when suddenly,
faster than rain,
it was already way
across the courtyard,
over the fence. Goodbye.
Never have I loved
anything running away
so much in my life.

If there was anything
to forgive – there wasn't –
I would have forgiven
you then.

Maybe Today

Eighth Song of Despair

Our dreams shiver
under a blanket of winter.
I keep wondering: when
will you remember how lovely
I am? I think of the princess and
her golden road. I even tell you
I am sad because
nobody has ever loved me
like I love you. You hand me
a shawl of comfort: how you do
love me, just not like that.

So spring will come again, if not
for us, at least for others. I dream
a memory of water on parched land.

I want to run the same path
each day; you want to explore
a different path. I want to hold
the same lover each day.
I wonder about you.

I want to learn from you. If
you don't get what you want
one day, you simply wait a day
or two and ask again.
You never know. Maybe today
will be different.

Maybe today I'll find the ladder
that will hold us
together.

Goddess

Ninth Love Poem

A woman who is loved
could live forever.

Every moment
a new waterfall, a stone
bridge in the symphony
of canyon wrens,
a kaleidoscope of trust
as strong hands catch
a fearless heart
across the glitter
of our circus tent.

Yes, everything, wild
roses, oh look, another
lizard, goldfinch, hummingbird,
and all the stars outlining
your infinity and mine.

Each morning an anchor
of fire, an angel stretching
to be something more.

My name is Love
and I want to go home.
This shouldn't surprise you,
though perhaps it does.

The Knight and the Lady of the Well

Ninth Song of Despair

Like a proverbial house cat never forgets
that she was once worshipped in Egypt,
a goddess never forgets.

An ancient story tells of a knight
(with long dark hair, of course)
who rides by a well, and a lady
offers him water in a chalice, and later
some wine. Soon they are married
and live in long and loving partnership.
She is a goddess it turns out.

One day the knight gets restless, asks
for leave to travel and find new adventure
and she says: Go. (What else could she say?)
So he rides off into enchanting distractions
and after some time he forgets.

Imagine being married to a lady,
a goddess, and you forget.

I will confess in my life I have
forgotten you at times while out
in the vast mesmerizing
world. I understand these things.

But my heart is mostly with her,
as she perhaps places a damp cloth
on the forehead of a feverish child,
or the trees around her grow tall,
unknown and unnoticed.

When will you remember? The well
has changed since you last saw it.
The wind tugs at its walls.
A goddess never forgets.

Freedom

Tenth Love Poem

Many years ago I knew I could be
happy in a cottage in the woods,
undisturbed. I wanted to just be
in love with God, the world, and,
if I found you, with you. And here
I am, in just such a place. Thank you.

Deer stroll by, lizards do push-ups
on the wall, quail glide along
like Country Western dancers,
never changing level, and I can
safely dream of a time when men
and women and children honor
each other without wounds
and complications.

Thank you for my freedom. When
I found out that the word "free"
comes from an ancient root,
"beloved, not in bondage,"
my heart did somersaults.

In the west the sun is sinking. Thank you
for the laughter in your eyes. Thank you
for the kindness in your eyes at dawn.

Thank you for freedom where I feel
devotion with the light of innocence
of one who has been honored.

Normal

Tenth Song of Despair

This then is the danger, when
the crushing heel of disdain
for women is so normal and
we live so awkwardly inured to it,
that we no longer even notice.

Indignant, I show a young woman
an ad for a cute nostalgic poster,
"Women Haters Club," printed
in a catalog designed to sell
primarily to women, and she
looks at me with large bewildered
eyes: What is your point?

I watch young women, proud,
intelligent, give in to condescending
flirtations. It works. It earns them
larger tips. I watch myself
simper and defer. It works. Yes.

Don't get me started on pornography.
Where do we live that it is pleasant
here, and normal, for a man to look
at women who look vulnerable,
for sure, and preferably dim-witted
as well? It is a bad, bad dream

in which I stumble naked on
the high heels of obedience, my finger
at my mouth, tongue lolling, while
the steady acid of contempt
keeps dripping and corroding me
like rust.

Beyond Reason

Eleventh Love Poem

I want to love you
beyond reason.

I read this dreamy story
of a woman waiting
for her husband with body and
soul spilling open, bathed
and scented with anticipation.
How treasured she must have felt
to let her love blossom like that.
I wish I could be her.

What am I saying? I used to read
more than a thousand and one tales,
many stirring with that
kind of love.

I told you one time I didn't learn
love from my parents, no.
I learned love from fairy tales.

But those are fairy tales,
you cautioned. No more
intangible than God or money,
though, I said, and we reasonably
live in cynical obedience to those.

I want to take you
beyond reason. If you follow
me into the fairy tale, I will
one day go to the forest with you
and we will sleep together
under the stars where we
belong. I promise.

Into the Mist

Eleventh Song of Despair

Reality is overrated. A mistake
is easiest with strangers, or even
better unobserved in solitude.

So I want to walk away.
There has been no welcome
for the only gifts I had
and what I wanted for
myself was often manfully
withheld: love, peace,
my circus dancer acrobatics
in a breathless world.

I have forgotten what I want
in life. I have lost desire.
I do not remember.
Let the sadness embrace me
of letting go of things I have
and also things I never had.

The mist is merciful.
The mist is undemanding.
So let me just walk off into
the curtains of forgiveness.

Not so fast, spirit says.
Don't you remember the corners
that have always turned
for you, unfastening
amazement? Yes, there always
has been new enchantment
when the dull mud broke open.

I will hang on a little while.
But it is good to know the mist
is there, white, rolling, daring,

extending secrecy, magnificence
and the temptation to be
remembered as one who walked
into the mist and didn't return.

The mist is forgiving.

The Timing

Twelfth Love Poem

I saw the perfect maple leaf
one day, spread in the sun.
I walked three paces, then
I turned to pick it up.
The wind had claimed it away.

Love, too, comes like a leaf,
a sunrise, or a rose. You cannot
say: Not now. Even a fox
would laugh if you tried
to schedule its trajectory.

All true lovers know this.
If necessary you steal time.
Love does not wait. Here
is my flame. Accept it while
it burns before it fades
away like a neglected muse.

There are other worthwhile things,
of course, friendship, commitment,
duty, but my love is fragile
like a rose, and also steadfast
like the sun, and matchless
like a maple leaf.

Let us not save each other
for special occasions.

Forgive Me

Twelfth Song of Despair

Forgive me.
At times I feel
I came to you too soon,
unfinished and unbridled
in my wailing disbelief
that all this glittering
and gifted world is turning
into energetic boredom.

Forgive me
for not being content
with loving myself, for
clamoring instead for
admiration from another:
You. Clearly
I am more needy than
the sun in luminous
indifference.

Forgive me
for being fed day after day
and still crying hunger.
Forgive my rage
at knowing so much
and not enough to break
these clammy fences
of irrelevance.

Forgive my chronic
unimportance, my sad
inability to comprehend
and make you comprehend
that I am as essential
as a cricket or a galaxy.

After the Forest

Thirteenth Love Poem

The moon is waning again.
The past is done.
The future can unfold.

I will meet you
at the crossroad as agreed.
I hope you are well,
my love. I yearn for
walking together again.

Once, as a wedding gift,
I wanted to give
you a language of joy.
I couldn't finish in time.
It was too dark
in the forest. The waterfall
was lovely, though,
and our vows took place
in silence anyway.
They couldn't compete
with the roar of wild water,
neither in beauty nor
in power.

Your threads go one way,
mine another now. Colors
mingle. Let us start
climbing. Should we fall, I pray
the weave will catch us.

Today I do not want to change
the world. I want to be with it
as is. Everything is possible.
If you were to invite me
to the river now, I would
come.

Acknowledgments

Many thanks to the editors of the literary magazines and anthologies in which the following poems first appeared, some in slightly different form:

Anima: "Poem Containing 'So,' 'And,' 'Such'"
Blue Lyra Review: "Bricks"
Blood and Roses: A Devotional Anthology in Honor of Aphrodite: "Goddess"
Borderlands Texas Poetry Review: "Sappho," "Escape Literature"
Caper Literary Journal: "Cathedral Garden"
Clear Poetry: "A Better Silence," "Lord of Lizards"
Crannóg: "After the Forest"
Cultural Weekly: "Archer"
Cyclamens and Swords: "Like a Prince," "Anxiety"
Desert Exposure: "Angel Loop, September," "Yearning to Praise"
Dissident Voice: "Ceremony"
Echoes from the Heart: An Anthology of Poetry for Peace: "September 11, 2001"
Focus: "The Tightrope Walker's Demonstration"
Grasslimb Journal: "Amo Ergo Sum: I Love Therefore I Am"
Harbinger Asylum: "The Book of Love"
Hawai'i Pacific Review: "Gratia Plena"
Improv 2008: Anthology of Colorado Poets: Peace War Love: "Valhalla"
The Independent: "Century Plant"
A Letter Among Friends: "A Fable of Leaves"
The Linnet's Wings: "Pine Siskin"
Mused: Bella Online Literary Review: "Grand Canyon," "Woman at the Crossroad," "The Alchemist," "Normal," "Patriarchy," "Back in the Woods," "The Timing," "Jealousy," "Freedom"
New Verse News: "When Lightning Strikes Men"
Le Nouveau Monde Vert: "That Day"
Olentangy Review: "Midsummer Night's Wake," "Crystals"
The Peregrine Muse: "Your Beautiful Eyes"
Poetry Saves: "Caged Light"
Poets Against War, Canada: "Pieta"
Raving Dove: "November 30, 2003"
Rose & Thorn Journal: "Neruda's Mermaid"
Salome Magazine: "The Wedding: Snow White"

Silver City Quarterly Review: "Desire," "Fairy Tale," "Into the Mist"
Spillway: "Xanthippe"
Three Sisters: "The Empty Pedestal"
THRUSH Poetry Journal: "The Storyteller"
Tuck Magazine: "Attention," "Excuses," "Maybe Today"
Whose Woods These Are: "Eurydice"
Wilderness House Literary Review: "Burning"
The Write Place at the Write Time: "The Wanderers," "Aubade,"
    "The Knight and the Lady of the Well"

*Cover artwork, composite by Diane Kistner; author photo by
Michael Schulte; cover and interior book design by Diane Kistner;
Haboro text and titling*

About FutureCycle Press

FutureCycle Press is dedicated to publishing lasting English-language poetry books, chapbooks, and anthologies in both print-on-demand and Kindle ebook formats. Founded in 2007 by long-time independent editor/publishers and partners Diane Kistner and Robert S. King, the press incorporated as a nonprofit in 2012. A number of our editors are distinguished poets and writers in their own right, and we have been actively involved in the small press movement going back to the early seventies.

The FutureCycle Poetry Book Prize and honorarium is awarded annually for the best full-length volume of poetry we publish in a calendar year. Introduced in 2013, our Good Works projects are anthologies devoted to issues of universal significance, with all proceeds donated to a related worthy cause. Our Selected Poems series highlights contemporary poets with a substantial body of work to their credit; with this series we strive to resurrect work that has had limited distribution and is now out of print.

We are dedicated to giving all of the authors we publish the care their work deserves, making our catalog of titles the most diverse and distinguished it can be, and paying forward any earnings to fund more great books.

We've learned a few things about independent publishing over the years. We have also evolved a unique, resilient publishing model that allows us to focus mainly on vetting and preserving for posterity poetry collections of exceptional quality without becoming overwhelmed with bookkeeping and mailing, fundraising activities, or taxing editorial and production "bubbles." To find out more about what we are doing, come see us at www.futurecycle.org.

The FutureCycle Poetry Book Prize

All full-length volumes of poetry published by FutureCycle Press in a given calendar year are considered for the annual FutureCycle Poetry Book Prize. This allows us to consider each submission on its own merits, outside of the context of a contest. Too, the judges see the finished book, which will have benefitted from the beautiful book design and strong editorial gloss we are famous for.

The book ranked the best in judging is announced as the prize-winner in the subsequent year. There is no fixed monetary award; instead, the winning poet receives an honorarium of 20% of the total net royalties from all poetry books and chapbooks the press sold online in the year the winning book was published. The winner is also accorded the honor of being on the panel of judges for the next year's competition; all judges receive copies of all contending books to keep for their personal library.

www.ingramcontent.com/pod-product-compliance
Lightning Source LLC
Chambersburg PA
CBHW070008100426
42741CB00012B/3149